First World War
and Army of Occupation
War Diary
France, Belgium and Germany

58 DIVISION
174 Infantry Brigade
London Regiment
2/8 Battalion
9 September 1915 - 26 February 1916

WO95/3006/2

Published by

The Naval & Military Press Ltd

Unit 10 Ridgewood Industrial Park,

Uckfield, East Sussex,

TN22 5QE England

Tel: +44 (0) 1825 749494

www.naval-military-press.com

www.nmarchive.com

This diary has been reprinted in facsimile from the original. Any imperfections are inevitably reproduced and the quality may fall short of modern type and cartographic standards.

© **Crown Copyright**
Images reproduced by permission of The National Archives, London, England, 2015.

Contents

Document type	Place/Title	Date From	Date To
Heading	WO95/3006/2		
Heading	War Diary of 2/8th London Regt Vol 2		
War Diary	Ipswich	09/09/1915	19/09/1915
Miscellaneous	From. O.C. 2/8th City of London Battalion The London Regiment	03/09/1915	03/09/1915
War Diary	Ipswich	04/10/1915	26/02/1916

WO 95/30062

174/54

Vol 92

WAR DIARY
OF
2/8th LONDON REGT.

Army Form C.2118

WAR DIARY
or
INTELLIGENCE SUMMARY

(Erase heading not required.)

Instructions regarding War Diaries and Intelligence Summaries are contained in F. S. Regs., Part II. and the Staff Manual respectively. Title pages will be prepared in manuscript.

Hour, Date, Place	Summary of Events and Information	Remarks and references to Appendices
7.11p.m. 9th Sept 1915 IPSWICH.	Eight piquets sent out to posts as Hostile Aircraft was expected. Piquets returned at 2 p.m. having seen nothing.	
10-15 p.m. 11th Sept.15 IPSWICH.	-ditto-	
9-15 p.m. 15th Sept.15 IPSWICH.	Two road piquets, one at 200 yards N.W.of Rly.Edge.on lane leading from IPSWICH to BRAMFORD and the other at Rly. Edge.on main BRAMFORD Rd. were sent out. They had nothing to report.	
5 p.m. 16th Sept.15. IPSWICH.	Transport inspected by O.C. A.S.C.	
6.20 p.m. 18th Sept.15. IPSWICH.	Practise Period of Vigilance announced.	
7.30a.m. 19th Sept.15. IPSWICH.	The Battalion entrained at IPSWICH STATION and proceeded to NAPESTORNE for Tactical Exercise and returned at about 5 p.m.	
3.20p.m. 19th Sept.15. IPSWICH.	Practise Period of Vigilance ended.	

30 SEP 1915

2/8TH (CITY OF LONDON) BATTN.
THE LONDON REGT. (P.O. RIFLES)

From O.C.2/8th City of London Battalion,
   The London Regiment.
To. Headquarters 174th Infantry Brigade.

<u>Training.</u> Each Company has been trained in succession daily in Trench Warfare, Relief, Attack, Interior Economy Etc. The remainder of the Battalion has been trained in combined Company operations (open warfare) The progress has been satisfactory.

<u>Machine Gun.</u> The trained Machine Gunners have fired sundry courses on Minature Range and at DISS with good results. The section is now furnished with 3 dummy guns for tactical training.

<u>Musketry.</u> All available trained men have completed their musketry. Recruits have fired Parts I. II. III.

<u>Grenadiers.</u> 100 men have received preliminary battalion training in Grenade work.

<u>Transport.</u> The battalion transport is approaching a good state of efficiency.

<u>Physical Training.</u> Each Company receives physical training daily for three-quarters of an hour and one company in succession daily bayonet fighting (final assault)

<u>Central Feeding</u> The Battalion is now fed at three centres This absorbs a large number of men for cooking and fatigues.

<u>Discipline.</u> Continues excellent.

<u>General Progress.</u> Satisfactory.

  Pay J. Reed
    Lieut. Colonel.
  Commanding 2/8th City of London Battalion.

IPSWICH.
  1.9.15.

Army Form C. 2118.

WAR DIARY
INTELLIGENCE SUMMARY
(Erase heading not required.)

Instructions regarding War Diaries and Intelligence Summaries are contained in F. S. Regs., Part II. and the Staff Manual respectively. Title pages will be prepared in manuscript.

2/8th Bn

Stamp: 58th (LONDON) DIVISION * GENERAL STAFF * 3 - NOV. 1915

Hour, Date, Place	Summary of Events and Information	Remarks and references to Appendices
IPSWICH		
4.10.p.m. Oct 4th 1915	1 Officer, I.N.C.O. and 6 men sent to DISS to an observation post for Hostile Aircraft.	This party has been relieved weekly.
7.35 p.m. Oct 13th 1915	Road Piquets Nos 8 and 9 were sent out.	
11.10.p.m. Oct 13th 1915	One, if not two, Zeppelins were heard by these Road Piquets to be proceeding in a N.E. direction.	
1.15 A.m. Oct 14th 1915.	One or more Zeppelins were heard. Weather fine and clear sky. No suspicious cars or lights were seen by Nos 8 or nine Road Piquets.	

(signature)

1247 W 3299 200,000 (E) 8/14 J.B.C. & A. Forms/C. 2118/11.

Army Form C. 2118

WAR DIARY
or
INTELLIGENCE SUMMARY

(Erase heading not required.)

Instructions regarding War Diaries and Intelligence Summaries are contained in F. S. Regs., Part II. and the Staff Manual respectively. Title Pages will be prepared in manuscript.

Place	Date	Hour	Summary of Events and Information	Remarks and references to Appendices
IPSWICH	Nov 2nd		This Battalion 437 strong took part in the 174th Brigade circular march. Left IPSWICH at 8.15 a.m. reaching DEBENHAM at 3 p.m. 2494 Sgt Warwick T. met with an accident and was taken to the Field Ambulance. Weather showery.	
	Nov 3	9a.m.	The Brigade proceeded to STRADBROKE via BUCKS HALL, BEDINGFIELD And HORHAM which was reached at 2p.m. One Rfn fell out. Weather showery.	
	Nov 4	9a.m.	Brigade proceeded to HALESWORTH via LAXFIELD and HEVERINGHAM. Dinners were had at WALPOLE. Six Rfn were sent back to IPSWICH as unfit to continue. One Rfn granted leave owing to serious illness of one of his family.	
	Nov 5	9a.m.	The Brigade proceeded to WICKHAM MARKET halting at 1.15p.m. for dinners at NORTH GREEN just N of PARHAM. WICKHAM MARKET was entered at 4p.m. A cook was accidentally hurt falling from a cooker and admitted to the Field Ambulance.	
	Nov 6	9a.m.	The Brigade proceeded back to IPSWICH which was reached at 2 p.m. The Battalion stood the test well and would have stood it better but for several cases of hard boots. These boots being very hard at the back produced several cases of badly blistered heels.	
	Nov 8	7.50 p.m.	Message received from 58th(London)Division via 174th Infantry Brigade that a big Air-raid might be expected shortly, and that this Battalion should be prepared to occupy its line at short notice and that all arrangements were to be completed for blocking of all roads emanating from IPSWICH in the sector allotted to this Battalion. All necessary arrangements were made but orders to take posts were not received.	
	Nov		During this month the Establishment of this Battalion has been reduced temporarily to 23 Officers and 600 other ranks.	

Lieut.Colonel
Commanding 2/8th City of London Battalion.
IPSWICH
1st December 1915.

Army Form C. 2118.

WAR DIARY
or
INTELLIGENCE SUMMARY
(Erase heading not required.)

Instructions regarding War Diaries and Intelligence Summaries are contained in F. S. Regs., Part II. and the Staff Manual respectively. Title pages will be prepared in manuscript.

Hour, Date, Place	Summary of Events and Information	Remarks and references to Appendices
Dec. 13th. IPSWICH.	A party of 2 Officers and 86 N.C.Os and men proceeded by Route March Route to BUTLEY where they were billeted in order to prepare the positions allotted to this Battalion.	
Dec. 17th do.	This party returned by March Route to IPSWICH.	
IPSWICH. 31.12.15.		Lieut. Col 2/8th City of London Bn The London Regt.

1247 W 3299 200,000 (E) 8/14 J.B.C. & A. Forms/C. 2118/11.

2/8 Batt. London Regt.

Army Form C. 2118

WAR DIARY
or
INTELLIGENCE SUMMARY

Secret.

Instructions regarding War Diaries and Intelligence Summaries are contained in F.S. Regs., Part II. and the Staff Manual respectively. Title Pages will be prepared in manuscript.

(Erase heading not required.)

Place	Date 1916	Hour	Summary of Events and Information	Remarks and references to Appendices
Ipswich	Jan 21		The first batch of Recruits joined under the Derby Scheme. HOP	
	-28	7.10 pm	The following message was received from 174th Infantry Brigade H.Q. "Aircraft reported heading for England. Be ready to turn out on receipt of further orders". HOP	
		9.40 pm	A further message was received saying "Troops will turn out for air raid". HOP The three Road piquets allotted to this Battalion were in position at 10.40 pm. HOP The firing party was in position at 11.40 pm. HOP No aircraft was seen or heard. HOP Troops left positions at 12 midnight.	

Hugh W. Priestley
CAPT. & ADJT.
2/8TH (CITY OF LONDON) BATT.,
THE LONDON REGT. (P.O. RIFLES)

Army Form C. 2118

WAR DIARY
or
~~INTELLIGENCE SUMMARY~~ SECRET

(Erase heading not required.)

2/8th Batt. Ln. Regt.

Instructions regarding War Diaries and Intelligence Summaries are contained in F. S. Regs., Part II. and the Staff Manual respectively. Title pages will be prepared in manuscript.

Place	Date	Hour	Summary of Events and Information	Remarks and references to Appendices
	1916			
IPSWICH	Feb 1		19 Recruits joined for duty	14aP
	" 2		11 " " "	14aP
	" 3		11 " " "	14aP
	" 4		9 " " "	14aP
	" 5		7 " " "	14aP
	" 7		20 " " "	14aP
	" 8		9 " " "	14aP
	" 9		16 " " "	14aP
	" 10		14 " " "	14aP
	" 11		23 " " "	14aP
	" 12		13 " " "	14aP
	" 14		23 " " "	14aP
	" 15		27 " " "	14aP
	" 16		9 " " "	14aP
	" 17		9 " " "	14aP
	" 18		2 " " "	14aP
	" 26		1 " " "	14aP
			205	

Capt J. Rees L.M.
Hughie Presley
CAPT. & ADJT.,
2/8TH (CITY OF LONDON) BATT.
THE LONDON REGT. (P.O. RIFLES).

www.ingramcontent.com/pod-product-compliance
Lightning Source LLC
Chambersburg PA
CBHW081514160426
43193CB00014B/2686